When

I

Knew

EDITED BY
ROBERT TRACHTENBERG

ILLUSTRATED BY
TOM BACHTELL

ReganBooks
Celebrating Ten Bestselling Years
An Imprint of HarperCollins*Publishers*

FIRST EDITION

Designed by Ph.D

Printed on acid-free paper

Library of Congress
Cataloging-in-Publication
Data has been applied for.

ISBN 0-06-057146-2
05 06 07 08 09 TP 10 9 8 7 6 5 4 3 2

PHOTOGRAPHY CREDITS

Pages 7, 35, 50, 70: Everett Collection
Page 52: General Photographic Agency/Getty Images
Page 21: Lester Glassner Collection/Neal Peters
Pages 1, 15, 37, 47, 57, 82, 90: Photofest
Page 69: Time Life Pictures/Getty Images
Page 29: Philippe Halsman/Magnum Photos
Page 45: Michael Childers
Page 100: Village People: Courtesy of The Island Def Jam
Music Group under license from Universal Music Enterprises
Page 101: *The King and I*: Courtesy of Geffen Records
under license from Universal Music Enterprises
Page 59: Wonder Woman™ and © DC Comics
Page 89: Robert Trachtenberg

1 **ANDREW FREEDMAN**, marketing/film industry 2 **DARIN JOHNSON**, public relations 3 **MAX MUTCHNICK**, co-creator/executive producer, *Will & Grace* 4 **STEPHEN ORR**, garden editor 5 **HOWARD BRAGMAN**, public relations executive 6 **JUDY GOLD**, comic 7 **RICK COPP**, writer 8 **RANDY SMITH**, marketing executive 10 **JENNY ALLARD**, head softball coach/freshman proctor, Harvard University 11 **LARRY WIEDEMANN**, talent agent 12 **DAN BARON**, marketing consultant 14 **ARCHIE GATLIN**, theater production 15 **MARC SHAIMAN**, stage and screen composer, *Hairspray: The Musical; South Park: Bigger, Longer, Uncut* 16 **SHAWN HENDERSON**, interior designer 17 **BARRY KARAS**, political fundraiser 18 **ROBERT E. BRYAN**, fashion editor 20 **JEFF JUDD**, makeup artist 21 **MICHAEL MUSTO**, columnist, *The Village Voice* 22 **MICHAEL FRANK**, teacher 23 **LESLIE BELZBERG**, film producer 24 **BRIAN HOWARD**, executive producer 26 **BRIAN LEITCH**, creative director/writer 28 **MICHAEL GRANA**, graphic designer 30 **DAN BUTLER**, actor 31 **ETTORE ZUCCARELLI**, executive photography director 32 **JON KINNALLY**, writer/executive producer, *Will & Grace* 33 **ELVIRA KURT**, comic 34 **JIM JOHNSON**, agent/producer 35 **KAREL BOULERY**, author/television/radio personality 36 **KATE NIELSEN**, writer 38 **MATT CHUN**, entertainment industry executive 39 **CHIP SULLIVAN**, publicist 40 **CHIP KIDD**, author/graphic designer 41 **STEPHEN FRY**, writer/actor/comedian 42 **TOM GILBERT**, magazine editor 44 **JOHN EPPERSON**, actor/writer/musician 46 **TOM BACHTELL**, illustrator 47 **MARIA BAUGH**, magazine editor 48 **ERIC MARSHALL**, interior designer 49 **KEVIN WILLIAMSON**, writer/producer 50 **ARTHUR LAURENTS**, librettist, *West Side Story*; screenwriter, *The Way We Were* 52 **GAVIN LAMBERT**, novelist/screenwriter/biographer 54 **RUSTY UPDEGRAFF**, restaurateur 56 **MAX KING**, interior designer 58 **JOHN BARTLETT**, fashion designer 59 **MATT BRUBAKER**, creative director 60 **TAMMY LYNN MICHAELS**, actress 61 **MICHAEL ENGLER**, theater/television director 62 **EDDIE SARFATY**, comic 66 **EDWARD SULLIVAN**, actor 68 **BOB SMITH**, comic 70 **MICHAEL SHULMAN**, writer 71 **ELVIRA KURT**, comic 72 **SIMON DOONAN**, writer/creative director, Barneys New York 74 **BILLY PORTER**, singer/actor 76 **MARK KUCHARSKI**, creative director 78 **JOHN McPHERSON**, attorney 80 **CHRIS MILLER**, manager 81 **JIM PROVENZANO**, author/journalist/playwright 82 **EUGENIO ZANETTI**, production designer/director 84 **TREBOR HEALEY**, writer 85 **ALEC MAPA**, actor 86 **MARGA GOMEZ**, comic 87 **GEORGE KOTSIOPOULOS**, fashion stylist 88 **BRETT FREEDMAN**, hair/makeup artist 90 **BD WONG**, actor/writer/director 92 **SEÁN Ó'MATHUNA**, actor 94 **DON SCOTTI**, producer 96 **JOEL WACHS**, president, Andy Warhol Foundation for the Visual Arts/former Los Angeles city councilman 97 **STEVE KMETKO**, entertainment reporter 98 **HARRIET ZARETSKY**, mother 100 **TROY NANKIN**, publicist 101 **SCOTT MILLER**, record producer 102 **JESS CAGLE**, magazine editor 104 **JAFFE COHEN**, comic 106 **JAKE LUBIN**, pharmaceutical industry executive 108 **DAVID SUGARMAN**, stage manager 109 **MICHELE BALAN**, comic 110 **DAVID FRANCIS**, novelist 111 **STEVE LEVITT**, screenwriter 112 **CHAD ALLEN**, actor 113 **JONATHAN ADLER**, ceramist/interior designer 114 **SUZANNE WESTENHOEFER**, comic 116 **OFER KAMIL**, caterer 117 **SCOTT FRANK**, advertising consultant 118 **ANDY TOWLE**, writer 120 THANKS

The stories in this book fall into four categories of no particular order: When I Knew, When My Parents Knew, When Everyone Else Knew, and the occasional (bonus!) coming-out story.

If this book can help just one person ... then I'm that much closer to getting residuals.

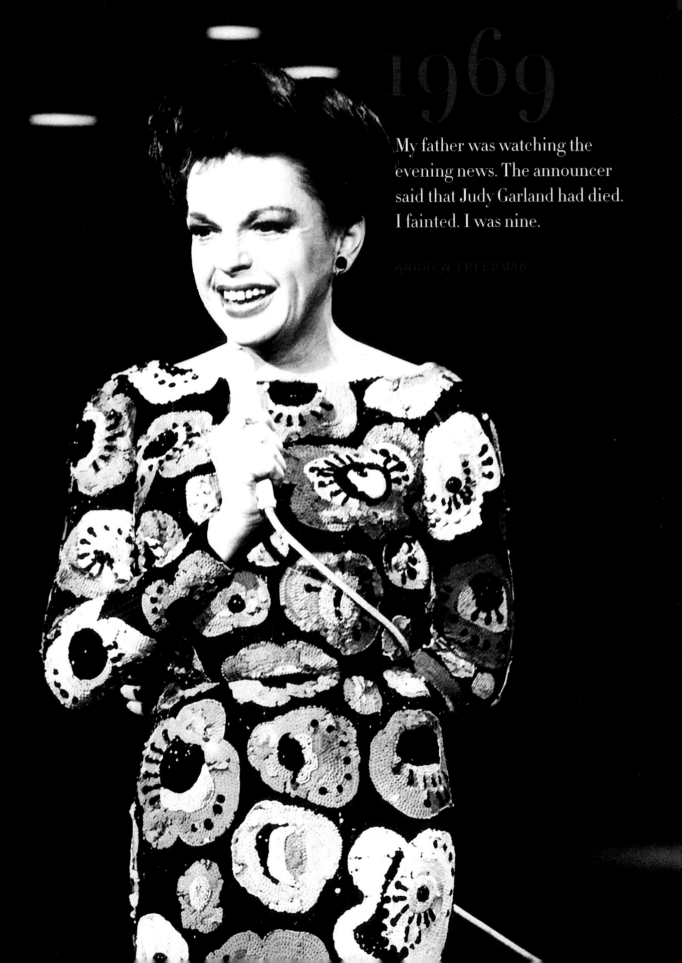

1969

My father was watching the evening news. The announcer said that Judy Garland had died. I fainted. I was nine.

ANDREW FREEDMAN

So my mother began the conversation, "Well, I was watching *Oprah* last week, and the show was about married men who turned out to be gay." A lump sank through my throat. She continued, "And Oprah said something that made a lot of sense to me."

"If you walk like a duck and quack like a duck, usually you're a duck," recited my mother. I quickly closed my eyes and prayed for an opportunity to escape her presence, but she had somehow found the courage. "Are you a duck, Darin?"

DARIN JOHNSON

I knew I was gay...

when I outgrew my mother's high heels.

MAX MUTCHNICK

1971, Abilene, Texas

STEPHEN ORR

My father was tossing a football with my brothers in the front yard. Seeing me sitting alone on the steps, my mother took my dad aside. "Dub," she said, calling my dad by his nickname, "I think Steve is feeling a little left out. Why don't you ask him if he'd like to play too?"

So my dad walked over. "Wanna throw the football some?" he asked.

"I'd really rather go pick flowers," I replied.

And we did.

My father, a former football coach, spent the rest of the afternoon picking flowers with me in a nearby field.

I knew I was gay when the most exciting part of my Bar Mitzvah was meeting with the party planner.

HOWARD BRAGMAN Congregation Beth Israel, Flint, Michigan, March 1, 1969

5

JUDY GOLD

I was a completely innocent eleven-year-old when my Hebrew school class came into Manhattan for the Israel Day Parade. You know how a parade always brings out all sorts of protesters and nuts? Well, for some reason, there was a woman along the route with a big sign that said, MY SON WAS A HOMOSEXUAL AND NOW HE'S NOT. HE WENT TO SEE DR. McSAMUELS 212-555-0125. Even in my innocence I remember thinking to myself, "I should be writing this number down...."

People always remember where they were when they heard the news that President Kennedy had been shot. I wasn't born until a year after it happened. But I sure as hell remember exactly what I was doing on that fateful day in 1977 when Farrah Fawcett-Majors announced that she would not return for a second season of *Charlie's Angels.*

RICK COPP

On our summer school field trip we went to Dallas/Fort Worth airport to see Braniff Airlines. The boys got to sit in the cockpit, and the girls got to see how the stewardesses changed their Pucci outfits mid-flight. On the way back home, our class went to a diner for lunch. There were twenty-five kids who ordered twenty-four burger and fry combos . . . and one fruit plate with cottage cheese. What can I say? It was what I wanted. RANDY SMITH

I knew in my twenties, when I kept waking up with women.

JENNY ALLARD

WHEN MY MOM TOLD ME ON THE PHONE THAT SHE AND DAD HAD JUST SEEN THE MOVIE PHILADELPHIA I KNEW IT WAS TIME. I ASKED HER IF SHE WAS SITTING DOWN. SHE KNEW RIGHT AWAY WHAT I WAS ABOUT TO TELL HER, AND IMMEDIATELY SHOUTED "...

OH NO,

BUT YOU WATCH FOOTBALL!" LARRY WIEDEMANN

grew up in Meriden, Connecticut.
On my twelfth birthday [1963]
my parents took me into Manhattan.
We went to Macy's. They gave
me five dollars and told me
I could buy any toy I wanted.
I took the money, went to housewares,
and bought a Fornasetti dinner plate.

DANNY BARON

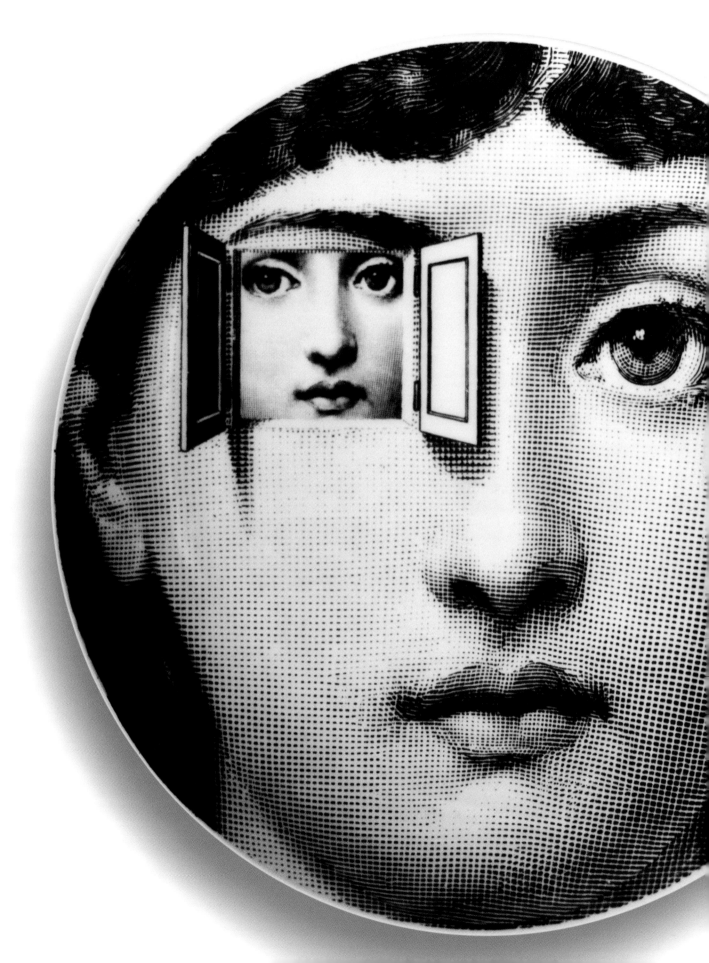

When I was six, my mother said to me, "Wait right here, I think I have something you'd be interested in." She went into the other room and came back with a pink feather boa.

ARCHIE GATLIN

I had a crush on Dick Gautier—he played Hymie the Robot on *Get Smart*. Hymie made me feel funny. I thought about him when I went to bed.

MARC SHAIMAN

eight

I suppose I knew I was gay when, at eight years old, I began hiding a purse under my bed ... filled with everything a sensible girl might need: cough drops and travel tissues. It was an old suede camera bag that I converted. Very chic.

SHAWN HENDERSON, 1969

Brooklyn, N.Y. 1953

I was eight years old, playing hopscotch out on the street. My dad and his friend Mickey Herzog are standing against Mickey's car watching me skip and hop around for a while. Mickey finally turns to my dad and says, "Ben, I think you got a problem."

BARRY KARAS

O f course I had known I was attracted to males since the age of five, but I didn't fully realize what that meant until one morning in the fall of 1962. I was in twelfth-grade government class at J.E.B. Stuart High School in Falls Church, Virginia, and the teacher, Coach Falls (who also coached the football team), was leading a discussion about queers. All of the government stuff bored him, and he preferred to talk about the things that were happening in the world at large, or right in our own backyard. It seems there had been a police raid on a house about a mile from school at a place called Bailey's Crossroads that was rumored to be a queer hangout. From there the topic of discussion moved on to the Seven Corners Shopping Center men's rooms and what a dangerous place they were to visit. The guys in the class were enraged by all this talk about queers, punching their fists in their palms and exclaiming, "If I could just get a hold of one of those guys I'd beat the ____ out of him!" Meanwhile the girls went to the other extreme, practically weeping with pity: "They are so sick, I feel so sorry for them, they need help." And as I sat there quietly, it dawned on me: they're talking about me! That being attracted to men meant you were a queer! After this traumatic realization I tried for the next year and a half to cure myself of this curse, turning off the TV during Olympic diving competitions, looking at the floor in the locker room, etc., etc. These were terrible sacrifices, which I regret to this day.

1967
I was lying on the floor of the living room, watching an episode of the *Tarzan* series. I kept sliding closer to the TV, sort of looking under it, trying to see under Tarzan's loincloth. Seven years old, go figure. JEFF JUDD

When the hormones first came at me at age eleven, I actually thought I could go either way—straight or gay—feeling so overwhelmingly sexual the options seemed enormous. But clearly I had entered my first self-delusion. As hard as I tried to get aroused by the women cavorting in bathing suits in travel agency brochures—even the ones with flat chests —they just didn't do it for me. I prayed to God to make me like these women—it would have made things so much easier—but even He had no interest in straight-ening out the little nelly. By the time *Tarzan* hit the tube, with hot, sinewy Ron Ely in the loinclothed leading role, I knew my place and was proud of it, becoming totally hooked on homo. Awkwardly enough, I kept it to myself for a while, but later made up for lost time like a truly crazed gay banshee. MICHAEL MUSTO

When I was ten

I would put on my mother's leather evening gloves—they came all the way up to my elbows. I would sing "Diamonds Are a Girl's Best Friend" into the mirror. One day my mother walked in and caught me mid-song—I tried to cover, screaming out, *"To the Bat Cave, Robin!"*

MICHAEL FRANK

My mother always dressed me—always. So in 1974 when I came home from college and told my parents I was gay, there was some drama. But the next morning when I came downstairs dressed in my usual jeans and flannel shirt, my mother, after seeing me in the identical outfit I've worn for twenty-two years, looked at me and said, "Aren't you looking a little

BUTCH

this morning?"

LESLIE BELZBERG

24

My mother had me tailed.

She did. She called her best friend Sheila, who was known for carrying a full flask of Kahlúa, her loud opinions, and her seemingly endless supply of Leroy Neiman paintings, to have her son Tom tail me in the West Village.

My mother had "found" a love letter written to me on the back of a math test with a very high score (which is what caught my mother's eye in the first place since math was not my strong suit).

Anyhow, I was visting my high-school flame Michael at his family's apartment when we stopped into the infamous corner store, Optimo Cigars on Seventh Avenue and Christopher Street, to buy some gum and wouldn't you know it, we were spotted by Tom as we innocently stepped out of the store and onto Christopher, "that gay street."

It was confirmed—my mother's best friend's son "outted" me and all because of a pack of Trident sugarless gum. There was nothing else she could do but sit me down that evening with my dad and ask me if I was "engaging in any homosexual activity." That was the most terrifyingly liberating question I had ever been asked.

Of course I said yes. I was free.

You don't just "know."
You know....
Then you know-know.
Then you really, really KNOW.

I *knew* when my fourth-grade teacher, Miss Mitchell, tried to comfort a delicate little boy. He had just been made to suffer through a particularly virulent bout of playground name-calling with this priceless aphorism: *"Gay, Schmay. You're born that way. It could be worse."* And then she hugged him. That delicate little boy was, of course . . . not me. The fact that someone else was taking the fall, being gayer than me, set me back several years on the know-know scale, impeding my prepubescent sexual development for years and years.

I would finally *know-know* much later than most, by a random act of chance. As a voracious and insatiable teenage shoplifter, I stumbled into the paperback book section of my local Kmart for a fresh kick and went to work, stuffing anything with a provocative picture or title down the front of my parka. John Rechy's *City of Night* and another really trashy book called *Us* (a sequel to *Them* and *We* and a prequel to *You*) were part of the haul, and I was in thrall. These books were stimulating. And I knew my favorite parts.

But I didn't really KNOW until junior high, grade seven to be exact, when I had blossomed into a chain-smoking wannabe badass delinquent, hanging out down by the railroad tracks, doing everything in my power to redirect and submerge my sexuality in my little Boxcar Willy caricature of masculinity. My seventh-grade teacher, Ms. Western ("Ms." was a new thing then, and I thought she was pretty cool to use it when no one else did) had asked me to stay late for detention one evening. We the detainees were asked to write an essay on why we were bad. I filled a few pages of foolscap with the things that made me unhappy about my life, the things at home, the things I wanted but that I suspected were missing, and the things I wished would go away. Ms. Western, who had one shrunken leg due to childhood polio, read my essay, and when the little tear trickled down her cheek, she said, "I hope I have a son like you someday." And I don't know why, but at that moment I thought of Miss Mitchell in fourth grade, and all the ways these two women had been a mother to me, looked out for me, took an interest in the unacceptable, strange, and "artistic" parts of me—the things you instinctively know, as a queer little kid, you're supposed to hide—and I looked into Ms. Western's pretty eyes with the little, knowing tear and strangely enough, that's when I really, really knew.

BRIAN LEITCH

When the Maid Knew

MICHAEL GRANA

1963: At ten, I was infatuated with Barbra Streisand. I bought black liquid eyeliner and would lock myself in the bathroom and practice drawing her Nefertiti-like eye extensions. One day the maid knocked. "Open up, I need the Comet," she said. "Give me a minute." I asked, both eyes fully done. "Open up now. I got work to do." "Just a second." I pleaded. "I don't have a second." She wasn't going away. It would take too long to wash the eyeliner off. I was trapped. I opened the door a crack. Our eyes locked as I handed over the Comet. "You should meet my nephew Bobby. You two would get along," she said as she turned back to work.

Daniel Eugene Butler

When I knew, REALLY knew, when it all came together in a cohesive penny-dropping Ah Ha! was while watching a production of *Boys in the Band* at Purdue/Indiana Theater in Fort Wayne, Indiana. I was a senior in high school. I'd been attracted to boys growing up, especially athletes and dancers. My friendships with boys were fierce—life and death affairs— but I thought that was natural, that everyone felt the same way I did. And if they didn't, they should. I went out with girls. I lost my virginity with my girlfriend. That's what you did. I never felt I was suppressing some deep need to be with a man. The terms *gay* and *homo* mostly referred to eccentrically silly or villainous characters in the movies.

But something shifted that night at *Boys in the Band.* (I thought it was a musical, that's how I'd gotten my two friends to come along, but that's another story.) The production was terrific. Funny and compelling and ALIVE! I remember watching the first scene where Michael and Donald are getting ready for a party. I didn't really take in what they were saying because I sat there, soul struck that here were two men talking with one another, in and out of clothes, intimate, comfortable, natural, and they were real, they were human, and I recognized something in them, a kinship, and I thought, "That is who I am. That's me." How great that one of the great loves of my life, theater, showed me who I truly am.

The seniors have now reached

I was officially told
when my wife
AND BOYFRIEND
sat me down and said,
"YOU'RE GAY!"

ETTORE ZUCCARELLI

As a kid, I became obsessed with the man on the Doan's Pills box. His back was so sexy. When my mom's supply ran out and she threw the box away, I went to the drug store and stole another. I stuffed it down my pants, where it's been ever since.

When I asked my mother when it was she knew, she looked at me with a mixture of bewilderment, defiance, and hurt—all shifty eyes, jutting chin, and furrowed brow.

I PRESENTED HER A LIFETIME'S WORTH OF EVIDENCE:
a bedroom full of train sets, Legos, every Matchbox and Hot Wheels car imaginable—but only one doll, a sad-eyed pixie whose long curls I chopped into a brush cut who now only wore construction-paper pants instead of whatever dress she came with; my own haircuts took place at the same barbershop my dad went to where everybody called me "Mr. Whiskers"; the only time I didn't scream, cry, bite, or kick my way into a dress was after my tonsils were removed and I was too groggy and weak to resist; I slept with my baseball glove through most of middle school; my first real bike was a boy's ten speed; during figure skating lessons I only practiced hockey moves with the other boys; I pretended I was Kristy McNichol ("I'll only answer to 'Buddy'") from the time *Family* aired until its cancellation; I worshipped Kate Jackson because she never missed a *Charlie's Angels* episode even when it got really bad; I went to see Jodie Foster movies again and again; I never had a boyfriend all through high school; they caught me making out with my first girlfriend in the basement of our house; I put rainbow flag bumper stickers on my car; I sat them down and said to them flat out "I am a lesbian"; and finally, she and my dad have been invited to my wedding.

No change in my mother, maybe some blinking. No answer either. I guess it all depends on what your definition of "knew" is.

17

I WAS SEVENTEEN WHEN I TOOK MY MOTHER TO A RESTAURANT TO TELL HER. "THAT GUY YOU'VE BEEN SEEING ME WITH—HE'S NOT JUST A FRIEND, HE'S MY BOYFRIEND." SHE STOOD UP. **"I'M GETTING SOMETHING FROM THE SALAD BAR— YOU WANT ANYTHING?"** AND THAT WAS THAT.

JIM JOHNSON

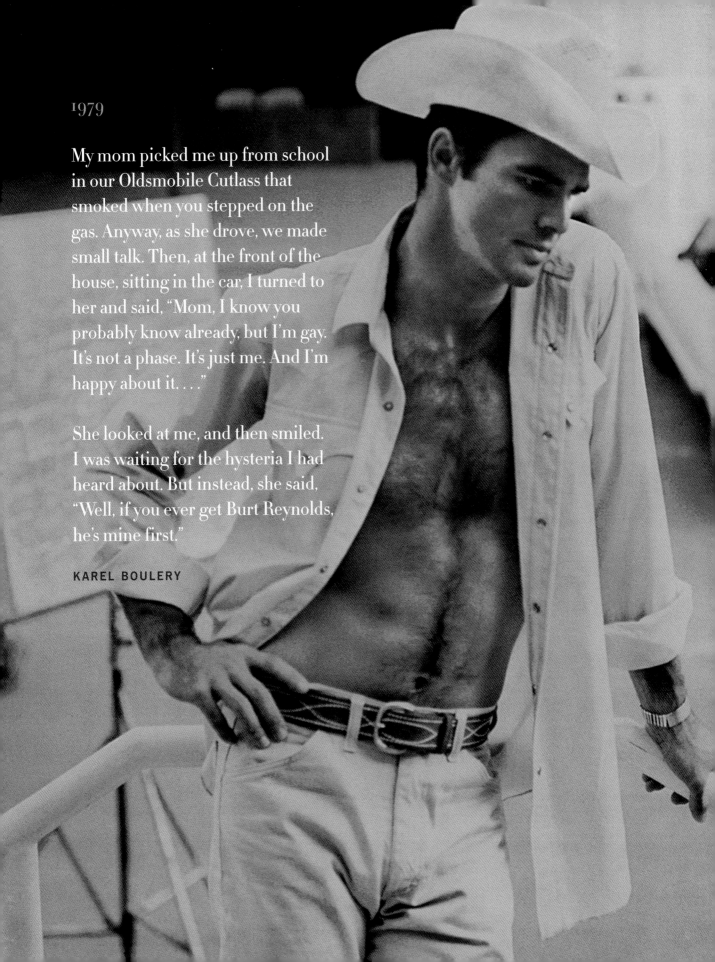

1979

My mom picked me up from school in our Oldsmobile Cutlass that smoked when you stepped on the gas. Anyway, as she drove, we made small talk. Then, at the front of the house, sitting in the car, I turned to her and said, "Mom, I know you probably know already, but I'm gay. It's not a phase. It's just me. And I'm happy about it. . . ."

She looked at me, and then smiled. I was waiting for the hysteria I had heard about. But instead, she said, "Well, if you ever get Burt Reynolds, he's mine first."

KAREL BOULERY

KATE NIELSEN

THE PARAMOUNT THEATRE

1965, Denver, Colorado

I was sitting next to my mother, munching on
popcorn, watching *The Sound of Music,* and I
wondered in my little five-year-old brain if it
was wrong to want to be Christopher Plummer,
a.k.a. Captain von Trapp. It was the only way, as
a girl, that I could imagine being able to be with
the beautiful Julie Andrews. . . . I made my
mother take me back to see the movie several
times that summer, which she was more than
happy to do as she just assumed it was because
I wanted to be a nun—not that I wanted to be
with a nun.

When
my family
moved into our
first home, my excitement
was oddly focused around four
plastic crystals dangling from the new
dining room chandelier. Fascinated by what
seemed to be priceless gems, I would often gaze
up at them while stretched on my tiptoes, longing for a
touch. But at age eleven, I was too short for the task. I was,
however, old enough to have stumbled upon the joys of jerking off. Not before long, those simple pleasures evolved to include
fantasies of my teacher, Mr. Lemyre, and sometimes Superman.
Horrified, I was convinced that it was the JO sin that had spawned
such queer thoughts. So I tried to abstain from the dirty habit, but every
night became a losing battle to the increasing perversion. Full of fear and
shame, I promised myself and God that as soon as I could reach those
plastic crystals, I would stop jerking off and stop being so damn gay.
One summer and a growth spurt later, I realized our new dining room
table under the chandelier had prevented my routine queer test for
some time. So pushing the table aside, I reached for the light
once again. I gasped. My wiggly fingers had shot right passed
the crystals, setting off a symphony of chimes. And it
was in that twinkling moment that I just knew.
This was me for good.
MATT CHUN

CHIP SULLIVAN

Tell me what happened.
I had to get my tonsils out when I was five.
And?
I refused to go until my mother took me to Saks Fifth Avenue to buy a traveling outfit to wear home from the hospital.
What was the outfit?
Madras shorts and a blue Lacoste shirt. It was the greatest.
What did your mother think?
She thought I looked fabulous, too.

I knew fairly early on. In fact, right after the doctor slapped me on the ass in the delivery room, I looked up at him and said, "Don't you think it's a little soon for that? I mean, you're totally hot, but let's at least have drinks first." CHIP KIDD

When I was born, I remember looking back up at my mother and saying, "That's the last time I'm going up one of those."

STEPHEN FRY

...eet kid,
...ood luck,
...he following
...o in school
...in choosing
ride when
time comes!
Love ya,
Debbie
(WAGGNER)

To a great kid,
see ya next year,
have fun this summer
good luck in '69
Kim

To a real
good ...
real ...
...

nice
the learning
this morning you
fun over the year have
are you always-
love
Sally '69
(EVERETT)

...
...
...
...
...
...

...fun in
a nice
every
body
and
good ...
9/69

It was indelibly, in blue ballpoint-pen ink, written into my seventh-grade yearbook:

"Your [sic] still a nice kid even though your [sic] a fairy. Phil." My pain upon reading it was so searing, so deeply felt, that I immediately knew his sentiment had permanently scarred my soul. I suddenly felt vulnerable and exposed, and, while I'd never acted on a homosexual impulse, I had no doubt he was right. I tried to laugh it off and even let my father read it, but his stricken countenance told me it certainly wasn't a joke to him. He never said anything about it to me, but the next day I learned he had discussed his grave concerns about my reputation with my older sister. The resulting shame and awkwardness I felt led me to never want anyone else to read that message, so I scribbled out the word "fairy," fashioned the resulting blob into something that looked like it might have originally been the word "Phillip," and wrote the word "nut" above the blob. My particularly deceitful finishing touch— a parenthetical little "sorry!"—was devised to turn my school "chum" Phil into a gentlemanly kidder who even apologized for making a big, unsightly scribble in my yearbook. It was the only apology I was to get. I've often wondered if he ever regretted writing that, especially in someone's keepsake.

1962, Hazlehurst, Mississippi:

Walking out of a Saturday matinee, I spied a poster for next week's attraction: *Gypsy* was coming to the Hazle Cinema. Mesmerized by the glamorous poster, I realized I'd have to coerce my mother into letting me see a movie that she might consider "dirty." Thinking fast, I reached out and took her hand. As innocently as possible I asked, "Mama, can I see *Gypsy* when it comes to town?" No response. I tore my eyes away from a Roz Russell lobby card and looked up. Only it wasn't my mother's eyes I was looking into. And it wasn't her hand I was holding. It was Carolyn Stout, a fourteen-year-old from the neighborhood. Dropping her hand in a flash, I turned to find my mother laughing at me, taking in the whole manipulative scene.

But if you've ever seen Lypsinka strip onstage you know how things turned out, because first matinee the following Saturday....

JOHN EPPERSON, A.K.A. LYPSINKA

TOM BACHTELL I remember going trick-or-treating in Ohio when I was 10 or 11. I couldn't think of a costume, so I just tried to look really cute. I had a toggle coat on, and my favorite pants and madras shirt underneath. And penny loafers! I was standing on a porch with some other kids when the home owners opened their door to hand out candy. They asked what everyone was and the shouts rang out: "Ghost!," "Pirate!" I had to think fast. **"WHY, I'M THE BOY NEXT DOOR!"** I said brightly.

How queer is that?

It was the spring of 1974.

I was ten years old,

lying on the floor of my grandparents' living room in Florida watching TV alone as Hank Aaron broke Babe Ruth's homerun record. I have no idea what it had to do with Hank Aaron or Babe Ruth or even baseball— probably nothing. It was fleeting, and wouldn't even be fully acknowledged for at least fifteen years, but it hit me like a ton of bricks and I thought, "Oh boy, what am I going to do now?" **MARIA BAUGH**

I heard this story

from my sister, years after it actually happened. At the time, I was fifteen years old. My father was in the middle of his weekly poker game with his buddies. The game got very heated and an argument broke out between my father and a friend of his. After one taunt too many, my dad lost his cool and shouted at his friend, "At least my wife's not fat and ugly." To which his friend replied, "Yeah, well at least my son's not a faggot."

The FISHERMAN, fifty-one, sits in his recliner in front of the television, flipping the remote, the volume blaring. Across the room, on the couch, sits his SON, twenty-seven, staring at him; anxious, something on his mind. After several false starts and what seems like an eternity, the son speaks.

> SON
> (quietly)
> Dad, I'm gay.

The fisherman hits the mute on the remote. The room goes silent. A long, agonizing moment. For the son, the world has stopped. He stares at his father, waiting for a response. Anything—the silence is maddening.

> FISHERMAN
> I figured it was that.

His son is confused.

> SON
> You figured *what* was that?

More silence.

> FISHERMAN
> Why we never talk.

Both men sit there, staring at the muted television.

FADE TO BLACK

KEVIN WILLIAMSON

When I was twelve,
I had sex with one of the kids on the block. We also went to the movies together and one day saw the picture called, *Let Us Be Gay*. Back then, "gay" merely meant bright, lively, merry, but for some unfathomable reason, whenever one of us wanted sex, we used the code phrase "Let Us Be Gay." I think we may have pioneered the use of "gay" to mean homosexual sex. More meaningful than a Tony or Oscar, but not quite worthy of the Nobel.

ARTHUR LAURENTS

**All this could only have happened
In a certain country** *(England),*
In a certain kind of family *(upper middle class),*
At a certain time *(beginning in the late 1930s).*

In those years our family often stayed at my grandmother's country house. When I was around eleven, my cousin, Maurice, who was around thirty, often came over for a visit. When we were alone, he would smile and beckon for me to sit on his knee, which I always did. Nothing, as they say, "happened," and we hardly spoke. But the silence implied a secret bond that I sensed without being able to put a name to it.

A year later I heard that Maurice had committed suicide. When I asked my incurably conventional parents what made him do it, they both hesitated. Finally my mother said, "He was one of those." I didn't understand, and after another uneasy hesitation my father said, "Maurice was different." Then the subject was firmly changed.

By then I felt different without knowing exactly why. But by the time I was fifteen, a charming teacher at school, who asked me never to tell anyone, had seduced me. He explained how closeted "different" life in England was, and how many famous people (writers, artists, sportsmen, politicians) were forced to live in a secret world. "But is there anything wrong in being 'different'?" I asked. "Of course not," he said. "Only in having to live that way or risk going to prison."

GAVIN LAMBERT

Two years later, as a student at Oxford, I became openly involved with Peter Brook, and the head of my college informed my parents. By then I had learned all the words for "different," of course, but none of them was mentioned when my parents were told that unless my "condition" was "cured" by a psychiatrist, I would never get anywhere in life.

I refused to be "cured," left Oxford, and went to live with Peter in London. When we broke up, my parents assumed—without ever saying so—that the breakup meant I'd been "cured." I saw no point in disillusioning them. I left England to live in Los Angeles, and when I went back for a visit, I realized how little the attitude of people like my parents had changed. I had been working on a film that starred the very talented, very heterosexual James Mason, and when my mother asked what was he "like," I mentioned that among other things, he was very fond of cats. My mother had an instant Pavlovian reflex. "You mean he's one of those?" Pretending not to understand, I told her that I was very fond of cats as well.

I remember I was about eight and it was Christmas morning. My three brothers and I tore into the mountain of presents. While they're pulling out Hot Wheels and baseball equipment, I'm digging for the long, thin boxes.

RUSTY UPDEGRAFF

I rip open the first one I find and scream "**All right!** Pajamas with matching robe … how cute!" And I remember the silent, confused stare from my brothers.

D o you think showing up for eighth grade with hair bleached the color of Tang is a benchmark for when everyone else knew? My aunt (the beautician) had promised me hair like The Beach Boys but had instead produced a young Hermione Gingold. MAX KING

(BEFORE)

(AFTER)

I knew at seven. My favorite pastime was shutting my eyes during *The Dating Game* and listening to the guys' voices to see if my pick would match that of the female contestant. I couldn't wait to grow up and be on the show

myself, picking my own bachelor number one, two, or three. JOHN BARTLETT

Wonder Woman™ UNDERO

Underwear that's Fu

MATT BRUBAKER

When I was six, my mother got me a Batman Underoos costume with a cape and mask to play in because my neighbors had similar Super Friends costumes. However, when I traded my friend Stephanie for her Wonder Woman Underoos costume, I was grounded and scolded.

The experience taught me two things: I knew that I was different, and I knew that I looked much better than Stephanie in that costume.

Girls'
Underwear
Set

ONE TOP & ONE PANTY

100% STRETCH POLYESTER
WITH COTTON
LINED CROTCH

6

TAMMY LYNN MICHAELS

When I was six I loved my first-grade
teacher so much I knew I would
have to grow up to be a boy so I could
come back and ask her to marry me.

I WAS IN 7TH GRADE

MICHAEL ENGLER

Twelve years old—and all the boys used to roll their sleeves up to the tops of their biceps in a tight, haphazard ring. One day I noticed an eighth-grader named Larry Klein with his rolled up completely differently. I practically swooned when I saw it. I'm not sure exactly how I would have described the feeling at the time, except to say that I felt as if I was discovering the secret to masculine, adult, sexy style. He carefully folded the cuffs of his shirtsleeves up over themselves only two or three times, so they ended up at the middle of his forearms, flat and relaxed. I went into a stall in the boys' room and copied him. I remember checking myself out in the mirror and feeling particularly cool. At the end of the day, my locker mate saw what I had done and derisively asked, "Why did you roll your sleeves up like that?" I said, "I like it. And Larry Klein wears his like that." He said, "Larry Klein is a fag." I felt completely ashamed but had no idea what he meant. The next day I was reading Ann Landers' column in the *Sun-Times* and saw a letter from a seventeen-year-old boy who said he was certain that he was a homosexual, and should he tell his parents? I had never heard the word before, but I instantly knew what it meant and that I was one, too; and that I would have to tell my parents one day, and show them how I rolled my shirtsleeves.

SECOND GUESSING GRANDMA

EDDIE SARFATY

I MAKE MY GRANDMOTHER CRY.

I come out to her and her fists close and her eyes fill up. She is silent for the longest moment and then, speaking through the tears, she astonishes me.

"It's that gym where you go, that's where they all are!"

Her assertion makes me laugh inside. How could she possibly know that? She's never been to my gym. How could my frail little grandma, a sheltered girl from an orthodox family, a woman who has barely left the house for the past thirty years, have any kind of insight on the subject?

The conversation continues with her becoming progressively more and more upset. She is perched on the upholstered green rocker from JCPenney, a half-finished afghan in her lap, and I am sitting Indian-style on the wall-to-wall carpet facing her. I'm peripherally aware of my mom and dad listening helplessly to the whole exchange as they pretend to wash dishes in the next room.

As a rule, when visiting my family I managed to find a million non-sexual things to talk about, which was a relief because when I was with my friends sex was the only thing we ever seemed to talk about. But this time Granny brings up the issue and continues pressing it until I have no choice but to come clean. She also confesses to having purposely avoided the subject of my sexuality until now but has finally decided to take the leap:

"Well, I thought that you were and I made up my mind that I was going to ask you!"

"Well, how do you feel?"

"It's a shock!"

She sheds more tears and my soothing accelerates to match her distress. I hand her a Kleenex and hold her hand. My mother, accustomed to taking charge in a crisis, takes advantage of my grandmother's poor hearing, tiptoes behind the rocker, shakes her head and mouths to me *"You shouldn't have told her. You shouldn't have told her!"* It is a big help.

With an evil stare I send her back to the sink and continue my comforting. Two seconds later the phone rings. I hear my mother pick it up and can tell from her voice it is my brother Jack in Chicago. I turn my attention back to Granny as my mother calls from the kitchen,

"Ed, Ed, pick up the phone!"

Annoyed, I yell back, "Not now, for God's sake!"

And then I hear my mother announcing as if into a public address system, "He can't come to the phone. He's telling Grandma that he's gay!"

And so I am outed to my brother and think, "One less call to make."

I spend the next hour or so quietly seated on the floor and then leave my grandmother to catch my train back to New York and the apartment I share with three other twentysomethings—all gay and in various stages of self-loathing. The incident is on my mind constantly the entire week. It is still on her mind too when I call home two days later:

"Hi Granny, how are you?"

"How do you think I am?"

Pin drops.

"What are you doing? Watching TV?"

"No, just thinking."

Crickets.

"Well, what are you thinking about?"

"What do you think I'm thinking about . . . ?"

Similar stressful exchanges occur on days three, four, and five.

Being the youngest, the favorite, and the only one who still lives close enough to visit regularly, I feel a special devotion to my grandmother. Our relationship is one of the most wonderful things in my life. She lived with us while I was growing up, my maturation coinciding with her decline. At the age of ninety-five (although she will only admit to ninety-two) her mind is sharp but her body is brittle. As time passes I find myself more and more in the role of the adult—keeping her informed, preparing her meals, and helping her into bed. The possibility that the bond between us could be permanently damaged is crippling to me.

After almost two weeks of tense, awkward phone calls I again go home for a visit. There is no reference to my revelation and the day passes more easily than I expect. It isn't until late evening when it even comes up. I am tucking Granny in—gently rotating her fragile legs onto the bed while I cradle her back and slowly lower her onto the mattress. As I smooth out the covers she brings up the subject that we have managed to avoid the entire day.

"So, you don't like a girl to get married?"

My body tenses, "No."

"You prefer a boy?"

I breathe deeply, "Yes."

She pauses and then says resolutely, "Well, then that will be your life and you'll be happy that way."

"Yes."

My tension melts away but returns when she says, "But it's not like making love with a girl. What can you do?"

I see where this is leading and try to head it off.

"Well, grandma, it isn't about sex. It's about who you love and who you care for."

She will not be deterred.

"Yes, yes I know that. But it's not like with a girl. What can you do?"

I dodge the question.

She presses.

I parry.

She asks again.

I change the subject.

She changes it back.

And finally after the fifth "But what can you do?" I blurt out, "Well, I have two hands."

"So what do you do, jerk each other off?"

I am stunned, horrified, and amused all in a single moment,

"Grandma!"

She laughs to break the tension.

She continues,

"You know I hear that some of the boys use the behind!"

I laugh to break the tension.

I toy with a couple of comebacks: "Wow, Grandma, what a great idea!"

Or, "Yeah some of us...er...some of them do," but settle for planting a simple kiss on her forehead and saying, "Goodnight."

After that our relationship is almost back to normal. She is totally accepting but it isn't clear that she understands the specifics of the situation. She knows I am gay but appears hopeful whenever I even mention a woman by name. She repeatedly asks my brother "What made him that way?" and confides to my mother her worries that I am destined to become a prostitute—a proposition that, given my precarious finances, occasionally worries me, too. My mother, who joined PFLAG* immediately after I came out, suggests giving my grandmother a copy of *Now That You Know*, a book that the group recommends and that I cynically refer to as *Everything You Always Wanted to Know About Homosexuality But Were Afraid to Hear*.

I pick up a copy for Granny.

Two weeks later I am home for a visit and to do some laundry. I see the book lying on the nightstand; the wrinkled spine and folded corners tell me it has been read. I turn to Granny who is busily working on yet another afghan.

"Hey Granny, did you read that book?"

The crochet hook stops, she looks up and says point blank,

"Yes, and it's disgusting!"

My heart sinks and my guard goes up. "Disgusting?"

"Yes, it's disgusting! It says that some of the parents don't love their children anymore."

SHE MAKES ME CRY.

* PARENTS, FAMILIES AND FRIENDS OF LESBIANS AND GAYS

1983

I was thirteen.

I had snuck away from my buddies. I was sick of building forts down by the creek. Those idiots couldn't take architectural direction and had no vision anyway. Marie and I were in her basement roller-skating to the *Xanadu* soundtrack. We were dressed . . . in wigs, skirts, and costume jewelry compliments of her grandmother. That afternoon I was wearing a tea-length number, long brown wig, and was in the middle of a spin, skirt twirling to the finale of *Xanadu*, when I looked out the basement window and saw my three guy friends staring at me, mouths open . . . frozen. Luckily they ran away laughing, otherwise I would have had to quit in the middle of my number.

THE TEST

My family received delivery of two daily newspapers when I was growing up in Kenmore, New York. The *Courier-Express* arrived in the morning while *The Buffalo Evening News* arrived around three-thirty or four every afternoon. My brother Greg's nickname for me was "Bookworm" and I read both newspapers every day. Therefore I can't recall which newspaper's advice columnist alerted me to the news that I might be gay.

It might have been "Dear Abby" in the morning or her sister "Ann Landers" in the afternoon. I read them avidly, as both columns covered many adult subjects that weren't commonly discussed by my parents. There might be a letter about infidelity in the morning or a note from a crank in the afternoon about the proper way to hang a roll of toilet paper. One day I read with particular interest a letter from a man who confessed that he was sexually attracted to men. "Confused in Cincinnati" asked if he might be homosexual but the letter also seemed to pertain to me; I was definitely confused in Buffalo.

I was in the ninth grade and knew that I found certain men sexually attractive but wasn't exactly sure about the differences between a heterosexual and homosexual. The border did not seem to be clearly marked.

I hadn't yet admitted to being gay because I hadn't completely ruled out that I was straight. But I was no dummy—and I'd observed that during a year of whacking off, no women paid a visit to my thoughts. It was clear to me that I should probably try to determine my sexual orientation. Being of a scientific bent—I still read every newspaper article about archeology, natural history, and astronomy—I decided to experiment with heterosexuality by using my penis.

I planned on going to our less-frequented upstairs bathroom with the objective of seeing whether I could bring myself to the point of climax by thinking about a woman. But which woman?

Looking around our house for a picture of an attractive woman, my eyes landed on the current issue of *Time* magazine.

It featured a cover story about a woman whom I had definitely loved since the first time I saw her.

With *Time* in my hand, I headed into the bathroom and after several minutes of strenuous concentration came to the conclusion that I wasn't straight. If I couldn't get off to Lily Tomlin then I would never be able to do it for any woman. It was a shock to realize that I was gay but I regarded the results of my test as valid and binding.

My relationship with Lily Tomlin didn't end that day, though. A year ago, I performed stand-up comedy at a benefit that she hosted in Palm Springs for a local AIDS organization. I was thrilled to finally work with the woman whom I always cite as one of my influences. My performance at the benefit went well— I killed —and at the end of the show, I found myself standing next to Lily Tomlin backstage. She smiled at me and said, "You're really funny."

After all those years, Lily Tomlin finally got me off.

BOB SMITH

I went to Choate Prep School. All the boys in my hall got *Sports Illustrated*. I seemed to be the only one with a subscription to *Women's Wear Daily*.

MICHAEL SHULMAN

ELVIRA KURT

3:00 a.m.

I was twelve and in the basement of our house at three in the morning. *The Trouble with Angels* was on again and I had to watch it despite the late hour, despite the fact that it was a school night, and despite having seen it so many times that I knew most of it by heart. I was so tired I kept drifting off but somehow always managed to wake up just as Rosalind Russell was catching Hayley Mills in some mischief. I woke up for that moment every time. As I lay curled up in the flickering darkness it hit me: this was no coincidence. My subconscious was rousing me for a reason, and not just to catch the best parts of my favorite movie. I had been awakened to the truth about myself and I suddenly knew who I was and what I wanted out of life: to be a bad girl who gets punished by a very angry Rosalind Russell.

SIMON DOONAN

In 1960 my parents took my sister and me to the Ideal Home Exhibition in London. I was eight years old. From the minute we arrived, I was mesmerized by the ultra-mod visuals. My burgeoning faggy sensibilities were intoxicated by the spectacle. Groovy chicks in spiked heels struck cutesy poses in kookily shaped chairs, while men in tight trousers giggled excitedly and made expansive gestures toward inanimate

objects such as throw pillows and Cornish ceramics. Were these young men visitors or exhibit personnel or both? I didn't know, and I didn't care. All I knew was that I was having my first encounter with flamboyant middle-class design aficionados. I had never seen groovy young guys like this before, except maybe in my blind Aunt Phyllis's knitting-pattern books. I was always more than willing to undertake the painstaking task of reading knitting-pattern instructions to Aunt Phyllis. It allowed me to appear saintly while gloating, unobserved, over the photos of chiseled young men posing, hands on hips, in tight adjacency. I was aware of homo-sexuality from an early age. My parents were acquainted with a couple of discreet working-class poufs, but they weren't good-looking like my knitting-pattern fellahs. And they demonstrated no passionate interest in decorative accessories. Their names were Ted and Burt and they shared a humble row house. Ted and Burt were quite ordinary. The only flamboyant or noteworthy thing about them was the gigantic electricity pylon in their backyard.

The flamboyant middle-class design aficionados at the Ideal Home Exhibition were a whole other genre from Ted and Burt. I watched enviously as they skipped and wiggled from booth to booth with their foulards flying, elbowing each other and gasping uninhibitedly at each new design innovation. They were like a strange, yet hauntingly familiar, species, a window into my future. I knew then that one day I would grow up to be just like them. I too would be a flamboyant middle-class design aficionado.

We didn't have much in the way of material things over at 6605 Brainard Street. But what we did have was the first floor of an old triplex with wonderful hardwood floors and wooden frames around all the doors. Apparently one day my stepfather felt he needed a change of scenery—so while I was at school he covered over ever inch of MY beautiful hardwood floors with SEMI-SHAG CARPETING!

BILLY PORTER

Oh, *I'm not done!*
He then proceeded to PAINT over every single wooden door and frame in the building WITH GLOSSY BROWN PAINT!

When I got home from school and saw what he was doing I threw my body across the last unpainted door frame, trying to save it from the machinations of my stepfather's pedestrian taste.

But it was not to be.... The final door was painted.

I boycotted the use of speech for weeks. I locked myself in my bedroom for a month refusing to partici-pate in what I called the SUBLIMINAL DETERIORATION OF MY NATURAL GOOD TASTE! *I was eight!*

I AM PROBABLY ABOUT TWELVE YEARS OLD. I gather all the kids in my neighborhood and proceed to sit them down in front of our family-room bar. I tell them that the game we are going to play is a surprise and that I just have to go and get something out of the basement to play the new game. In the basement I gather all of my father's bowling trophies and proceed to walk up the stairs when I run into him. "Where are you going with all those old trophies?" he asks. "I have all my friends upstairs and we are playing Academy Awards," I reply. My father just rolls his eyes.

MARK KUCHARSKI

Jack McPherson
1967
LEADERSHIP

I don't like baseball or softball; never have, never will.

But for years, as a little boy, I had to accompany my family to the Little League field and Bobby Sox softball field and watch my brother and two sisters play their games. My mother (Dad was often overseas with the navy during those early Vietnam War years) usually let me sit in the car and read, though she occasionally made me sit in the bleachers with the other families in order to promote—well, who knows what she hoped to promote.

When I was about ten or eleven (and Dad was on yet another tour of duty), my mother finally agreed to let me stay home by myself. I was in heaven. I would put the cast albums to *Carousel* or

Oklahoma or *West Side Story* on the hi-fi, turn the volume up loud and dance all over the house. Or I'd play *Swan Lake* or *The Sleeping Beauty* and pretend I was a great ballet dancer just like the men and women I saw on television. Around that same time, I was lucky enough to attend *Swan Lake* performed live by the Royal Ballet/Covent Garden. Even better, my mother or my Aunt Mary purchased the gorgeous color souvenir brochure for me; I spent hours and hours poring over the dancer biographies, staring at the production photographs, and reliving that wonderful night at the theatre.

One evening, as *Swan Lake* blared in the background, the doorbell rang. I took a last leap over the coffee table, turned down the volume, and ran to the door. Our former babysitter, Judy, was standing on the porch with her new husband, a young, handsome naval officer named "Guy." They were in the neighborhood and had stopped in to say "hi" to my folks. Judy was somewhat surprised to find me at home alone, and I immediately launched into telling her about seeing *Swan Lake* and how I was listening to the music and re-imagining the show. I showed her the colorful program and described the story and costumes. I'd spent some time drawing my ideas for sets and costumes and I grabbed my drawings and showed her those as well.

While Judy and I spoke, Guy looked at me. He pushed the drawings around on

the table. He paged through the brochure. At some point, he interrupted and said, "You like this stuff? The dancing and the music? You'd rather be here at home by yourself instead of at the baseball field? And does your dad know you like this stuff?" I said "sure" or nodded my assent. But the look on his face—which I recall to this day—did me in; it was a mixture of bemusement, disapproval, and disgust. The face said it all: "Jesus, the kid's a sissy."

It was like someone turned a switch off inside me. I told them that Mom and the other kids would be home in an hour or so, then I began gathering up my drawings. I stopped talking and only answered questions asked of me. Judy had known me for years, and I suspect she knew my feelings had been deeply hurt. She said they'd come back some other time and then they left. I turned off the music and put the program and my drawings in the bedroom I shared with my brother.

When my family came home, it was after dark. My mother found me sitting in the living room, curled up in a corner sofa. "Are you okay, Jack? Why are you sitting here in the dark? Did you fall asleep?" I told her I must have fallen asleep, though I hadn't. I'd been awake the whole time, thinking, as only a child can, "Why didn't he like me? What's wrong with me?"

JOHN McPHERSON

79

I knew for sure on Christmas morning, 1974. I was five years old. My sister Liz and I each had a wrapped present that was exactly the same size. It was her turn to open; she tore the wrapping off a beautiful Barbie camper. It was a magical bright orange, with little dishes and cookware. After what seemed an eternity of photographs and fussing over my sister's new camper, it was my turn to open. I grabbed my matching gift. Visions of my sister and me taking Ken and Barbie on long lazy vacations around the back-yard in our matching motor homes filled my head. I tore through the wrapping paper, I could see the box, yes, it was a matching camper, but wait, mine wasn't orange and lovely, it was camouflaged and ugly and it wasn't for Ken and Barbie, it was for G.I. Joe. It didn't have cute dishes and service for two; it had binoculars and walkie-talkies. I was devastated. I cried. I was gay.

MEN JIM PROVENZANO

On summer trips to Brookside Pool, my brother, sister, and friends usually went with us. One time, for some reason, I went with only my mother. At the doors to the men's and women's changing rooms, she asked if I needed help, and said I should change in the women's room, since I was only six years old. At that moment, two sun-bronzed lifeguards passed, laughing and peeling their shirts off, on their way to the door with the **MEN** sign over it. I waved to Mom, following the lifeguards, and said, "I'll be okay."

nineteen fifty-seven

I was eleven years old.

Remember, this is Buenos Aires, Argentina, and I wasn't a sissy boy or anything like that, but I went to the movies to see *Sayonara*, starring Marlon Brando. I was really enthralled—the story, the setting, the geishas—all of it—I was gone. And when Brando leaned over to kiss Miyoshi Umeki, I realized that I was leaning over in my seat at the exact same angle Miyoshi was to receive Brando's kiss. . . . That was really something to me, but then again I also found myself walking out of the theater with shorter, geisha-like steps, so . . . EUGENIO ZANETTI

It was getting late. We both liked poetry and drinking and were generally depressed, and so had once again ended up at our favorite dive bar, talking about poetry, and then reading some back and forth to each other. I remember the place stunk like Pine-Sol and mold and we looked more dilapidated than ever. We'd gotten pretty looped and when he asked me that question I'd been lying about for years, I looked down at the page of Eliot I'd been reading:

HURRY UP PLEASE, IT'S TIME/HURRY UP PLEASE, IT'S TIME

I leaned across the table and kissed him on the mouth.

TREBOR HEALEY

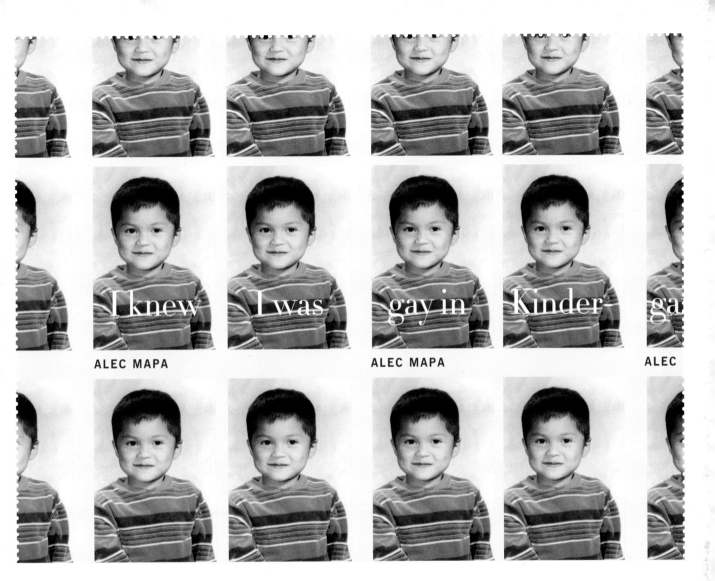

I knew I was gay in Kinder-ga

ALEC MAPA

ALEC MAPA

ALEC

I was the only boy in class who cared about picture day. I agonized over what to wear. I was going to wear a white short-sleeved shirt with a black clip-on tie, but at the last minute decided to go with a baby blue pullover. It was less formal, broke with tradition, and the open collar de-emphasized the roundness of my face.

I was at school lining up to have my photo taken and I was very nervous. We'd all been given black plastic combs and I couldn't stop raking it through my hair. It was my first photo shoot and I just wanted to get it right. It was finally my turn to have my picture taken, the photographer sat me down on the stool and at the very last minute I decided to pose. I looked straight into the camera, aimed my shoulder at the lens, tilted my head to the side and FLASH! I looked like Cindy Brady trapped in the body of a little Asian boy. My father was furious.

The first time I ever saw lesbians I was just a kid. They were on the David Susskind show. My mom was watching it downstairs with the volume low. But I could hear it with my bedroom door shut and my radio blasting because I had already developed homosexual hearing. I joined my mother in front of the TV. For her benefit I looked disgusted and shook my head in disapproval. Secretly I was mesmerized. The three lesbians were disguised in raincoats, dark glasses, and wigs. I believe it was the chance to wear a wig that made me want to be one. **MARGA GOMEZ**

1976

I was watching a James Bond movie on the TV in my parents' bedroom—at least I think it was a Bond film.... There's a scene where 007 forcefully embraces his Bond girl. He then proceeds to cut the straps of her evening gown so it falls to the floor leaving this gorgeous woman standing stark naked right in front of me. Of course, this was TV pre-cable and she wasn't really naked, but I was eight and this was supposed to be hot stuff for me. But all I can remember thinking was, "Why did he have to go and ruin such a beautiful dress?"

GEORGE KOTSIOPOULOS

My family—Mom, Dad, sister Dee Dee, and I—were in the family room watching television. Dee Dee was making up one of those big Barbie heads while she watched, and she could not do it. I was sitting on the edge of my seat, trying to concentrate on the program, but I was losing my mind; she was doing everything wrong. Finally, I saw the last straw—I couldn't help it anymore—I screamed out, "Dee Dee! You can't part her hair on the side! She has a heart-shaped face!" BRETT FREEDMAN

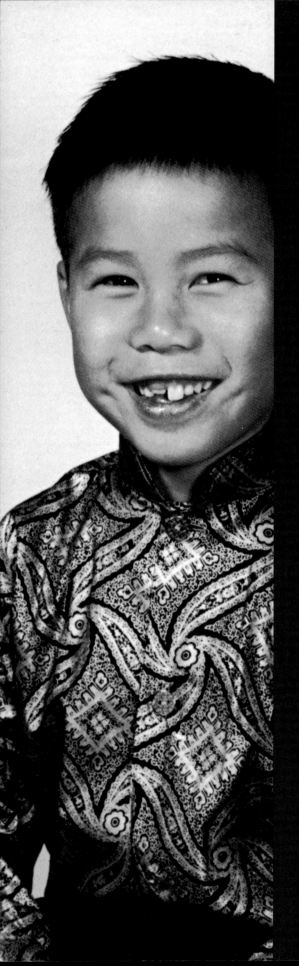

the ballad
of baby b

BY

BD WONG

This is the ballad of baby b
Checking out boys by the time he was three
Something was up from way far back as then
Now oddly enough, baby b's into men

Come out, come out, whoever you are!
Come out, politician, or big broadway star!
Come out to your parish! Shoemaker to elf!
Am I going too fast? Just come out to yourself!

Baby b (d) was bayarea born
(Yes, home of the palace of fine arts, and porn)
Frisco had chinatown, castro, and bradley
Between these he grew up both sadly and gladly

Come out, come out, wherever you be!
Come clean in kentucky! Come march in dc!
Come up in a lilac canaveral cape!
Come down in a hot houston mineshaft, you ape!

Way back of the library, hidden (at nine)
Our hero sat reading; day, night, rain, or shine
Anatomy books, color plates of rodin:
Hypnotic'lly struck by each image of man

E'en though he was wee,
        he could tell from those books
That he yearned for the dudes
        with great bodies and looks
Even pre-adolescent,
        watching this man or that man
(He eas'ly got off watching robin and batman)

Come out, come out, wherever you've been!
Be you master of dungeon!
        Be you new to the scene!
Life passes us by, life's end can be bitter
If you fail to heed my advice, and consider:

Come out, come out, however you please!
If gay indeed *he's*,
        Then the *day* he must *seize*!
No one is exempt! Not a queen bee or peasant!
No more waiting! No waffling!
        No time like the present!

He waited two decades until he decided
To spill to his parents, his conscience divided
The answer came calling, in form of a beau
To help him say,
        "mom, here's what I have to show"

This guy that he loved, made it seem kind of right
Softened the blow (god forbid they should fight)
Mother was worried, but father was not
(He said, "just as long as you love him, so what?")

As years tumbled by, the pair had a child:
Saw many a setback (and papers were filed)
One wonderful night, like a gay flag unfurled,
Two guys (with two gals) brought
        new life to this world...

So, bursting with pride, bd—a/k/a brad—
Proclaimed to the world how he now was a dad
Writes a book
        (a self portrait of pop-hood, he draws it);
And feeling no pain, out he comes
        from the closet!

Come out, come out, it's just swell, take a look!
(You don't even much need
        to have written a book!)
Stand up! Put your hand up! Upset someone, dear!
It will all be okay, there is nothing to fear!

Fast forward the tape, life is furious and funny
How things will turn out you can't guess,
        or bet money
Just go where life takes you, no matter the season
Remember that all things occur for a reason

To say it succinctly, bd made some choices
A parting of ways, a finding of voices
Life's grateful, God-awful,
        God bless-ed and gambl-y
But *with* that swell guy,
        he's re-structured their fam'ly

And that, in a nutshell, is just about it
Since he said "This is me,"
        how his candle has lit!
With nods of respect to his son's other dad:
Though not what they hoped,
        life's *far* from so bad ...

Come out, come out, you son of a bitch!
Don't think about whether you catch, or you pitch!
Just do the right thing and cross over the line!
Let me tell you, I know that the water is fine!

This was the ballad of baby b
Wasn't quite right till he said, "This is me"
All of his life, never felt he was winning
But now it seems life is just barely beginning ...

I'm twelve and I've organized a covert "dress-up" party for the gang. My parents are at the store and won't be back for hours. They would not be impressed with this. Malachy is negotiating his way, in size thirteen loafers. Anna has on layers of costume jewelry and a yellow silk scarf. Francis is fussing with an apron and a rolling pin and Gavin is futzing with a pack of cheap cigars and a smoking jacket. Excitement has reached a fever pitch when I hear Dad's car pull into the driveway.

"They're back," I scream and within seconds the room clears. Everything is replaced and we are back in position; the picture of innocence. We are safe; we had run this drill before. Mom opens the living room door and looks around. She stops and glares at me. My father enters, looks at me, sighs and shakes his head.

"Have you been playing with our clothes, again?"

"No," I say, and as I shake my head defiantly I feel the faint netting brush across my face. Everyone is staring and I blush. Gavin points and Francis giggles. My Dad shakes his head—again! Mom walks over, stands in front of me, and removes her wedding veil from my head.

BROOKLYN

1956

I was seven. My father took me and my family to see Cecil B. DeMille's THE TEN COMMANDMENTS with Charlton Heston at Radio City Music Hall. We got there late and had to sit in the first row looking straight up at a perfect row of Rockettes kicking over our heads. That is when I finally realized what God put me on this Earth to be when I grew up: a Rockette.

DON SCOTTI

When I first ran for public office in 1971, I was petrified someone would know I was gay. After all, it was 1971, and at that time not a single openly gay person had ever been elected to public office anywhere in the United States. Then one day I looked up at one of my billboards on the busiest thoroughfare in my district and I saw the word FAG spray-painted all over it. And I thought: "Oh well ... so much for the closet!"

JOEL WACHS

STEVE KMETKO

Maybe it was when I planned the marriage to my high-school sweetheart—string quartet, candlelight sconces, amazing flowers, choice of rings, design and execution of the wedding dress. It was only later—like immediately later, that I realized:

1 I've made a terrible mistake.

2 Wasn't the wedding fabulous!

3 How am I going to get it up?

HARRIET ZARETSKY

1959

When my name was Hadassah Rosenblum and my father was an Orthodox rabbi, a friend from high school took me to a gay bar in the Village. I didn't know what to expect or exactly what was behind those doors, but I knew a lot of gay bars were mafia run back then. It had red lights everywhere and was real sleazy, but pretty soon a handsome man came over and handed me a RED ROSE with such intensity ... at the same time that I was feeling thrilled and flattered, I was also feeling that this was no man; it was actually a really butch woman named Bobby Alvino.

Then it hit me—that made it even better.

Although it's very sweet that my mother always gave me a present on Valentine's Day, it does seem odd that two years in a row she gave me albums by the Village People....

ORIGINAL CAST ALBUM featuring Members of the New York Production

RODGERS and HAMMERSTEIN
present

Gertrude
LAWRENCE

in A New Musical Play

The King and I

YUL BRYNNER

RICHARD RODGERS

Book OSCAR HAMMERSTEIN II

with

DOROTHY SARNOFF • DORETTA MORROW • LARRY DOUGLAS

Directed by JOHN van DRUTEN

ORCHESTRATIONS BY ROBERT RUSSELL BENNETT
MUSICAL DIRECTOR, FREDERICK DVONCH

OVERTURE • I WHISTLE A HAPPY TUNE • MY LORD AND MASTER • HELLO, YOUNG LOVERS • MARCH OF THE SIAMESE CHILDREN
A PUZZLEMENT • GETTING TO KNOW YOU • WE KISS IN A SHADOW • SOMETHING WONDERFUL
SHALL I TELL YOU WHAT I THINK OF YOU? • I HAVE DREAMED • SHALL WE DANCE?

Printed in U.S.A.

DECCA
BROADWAY

> I suppose I was a musical prodigy, but… it was my third birthday, and my copy of the soundtrack album of *The King and I* had broken. Hearing of my heartbreak over the loss, my aunt bought me a new copy. I remember unwrapping it, instantly filled with disappointment. "This is the show! I wanted the movie soundtrack! The orchestrations are so much better!"
>
> **SCOTT MILLER**

Citrine

Topaz

Zircon

MY DAD WAS A
BIG, **TALL** TEXAN
WHO CO-OWNED
A FEEDLOT.

Ruby

Opal

Garnet

Onyx

Amethyst

Moonstone

When I was in fourth grade, he told me that about two dozen of the cattle belonged to me. They would be slaughtered, and the proceeds would be put into my savings account. I asked if I could give the cattle names, and he said yes, thrilled that his son was suddenly more interested in the feedlot than *Bewitched* and decorating the house. The next day as we drove to the feedlot, he asked me if I had come up with any names. I told him I had. I was going to name each of the cattle after precious stones.

JESS CAGLE

Sapphire

Diamond

Emerald

THE DOCTOR IS OUT

JAFFE COHEN

I never went to medical school, but when I was a kid in Levittown, Long Island, I did play doctor with my next-door neighbor. First of all, let me change his name to Johnny Johnson, not so much as to protect him from being labeled gay, but rather to avoid a medical malpractice suit if he ever realizes I wasn't a twelve-year-old proctologist. Many were the times my proud parents caught me thumbing through the medical dictionary looking for any conditions that could only be treated with the patient's pants pulled down around his knees. Looking back I have to ask myself why this cute kid—half Italian, half Irish—regularly submitted to these procedures. Maybe an uncle had told him Jews make the best MD's. . . .

Now the same year I was providing health care for Johnny, I was also studying for my Bar Mitzvah with the Cantor Boris Fisch. Being a bright kid and eager to please, I soon became one of Fisch's favorite students and he would often encourage me to continue my studies after my Bar Mitzvah. I was conflicted. As much as I wanted to please the kindly old cantor, going to Hebrew high-school nights and weekends would have severely cut into the time I'd been spending studying Johnny Johnson for any curvature of his spine.

But when did I first know I was gay? For me it was about six months into my medical career, and I couldn't tell you the date or even the time of year but I could tell you the exact spot where, like the Buddha himself I achieved complete realization of my exalted status. It was on a crack in the sidewalk midway between my house and the Johnson's.

I'd been in a chivalrous mood that night and decided to walk my neighbor home, a journey of about forty feet and while returning, it suddenly occurred to me—not that I was gay but that I'd always been gay and that I would stay gay. Before Johnny there'd been a whole squadron of us boys willing to tickle each other's wieners in backyard pools. It was like we were all auditioning for a Merchant Ivory film set on Long Island. But one by the one, the old gang had taken up with girls from adjacent neighbor-hoods and it would only be a matter of time before I'd lose Johnny to the head of the pom-pom squad. This all came to me in a flash.

Saddled with this sudden knowledge, what could I do but fall to my knees and pray to the God of Cantor Fisch? "Adonai!" I cried (for that's His name in Hebrew). "If there's anything wrong with being gay, I want you to give me a sign!" Nothing happened. Guessing that he might be on the line with someone else I waited for him to get back to me. Nothing happened. I counted to ten. One one thousand. Two one thousand. Three one thou-sand. By the time I got to eight I was feeling pretty annoyed because *Green Acres* was about to begin on TV and I didn't appreciate being kept waiting. Finally at ten I got to my feet, took a deep breath and went home with a big smile on my face because I'd managed to kill two birds with one stone. To this day I haven't suffered a moment of guilt about being gay and after being Bar Mitzvahed I bagged any idea I had of going to Hebrew high school. From that moment on, my time would be my own.

My sister, Lori, her best friend Sara, and I would often play Miss America Pageant in our Arizona backyard. The game always coincided with the beginning of summer when my mother would get new beach towels, which we would use as evening gowns. Lori and I always forced Sara to use last season's beach towels. She never won the evening-wear contest.

LORI WAS ALWAYS MISS TEXAS, SARA WAS MISS CALIFORNIA AND I, WANTING TO BE DIFFERENT, WAS MISS RHODE ISLAND.

One afternoon, my father ran out of gas while mowing the lawn. I looked at the half-mowed lawn and saw the perfect pageant runway. "The rows are perfect for us to stop at the end and wait for the girls from other states to come down," I exclaimed. How anyone could not have known I was gay is beyond me. But I do know that Miss Rhode Island holds the record for most consecutive wins in the Miss America Pageant in my own backyard.

IT'S HARD TO PINPOINT THE MOMENT I KNEW I WAS GAY.

I'm not sure there was ever a time I didn't feel this way. But I do remember the moment when I found out what it was called and that there was something "wrong" with it. I was out for breakfast at Friendly's with my grandmother. The waiter had just taken our order and walked away from our table in his blue-and-white checkered polyester uniform. My grandmother told me, "I think he's a little queer," as she looked off at the wall over my head and fingered her oversized earrings. I'm not sure I knew what she meant, but I did know that the waiter and I shared something essential and that she thought there was something wrong with it. We ate breakfast and then completed our Saturday morning ritual: proceeding to the beauty parlor where I watched her get her weekly wash and set.

DAVID SUGARMAN

My grandmother raised me.

When I told her that I was a lesbian, she said,

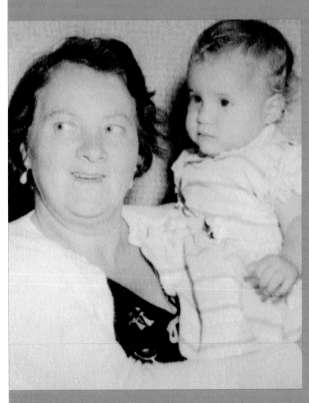

"No you're not, you're Romanian. On your father's side!"

MICHELE BALAN

DAVID FRANCIS

I was four

when I traveled with my parents to the Feed Islands, north of New Guinea. My father's best friend Graeme had a coffee plantation there. When we arrived and walked up from the boat I couldn't help noticing Graeme in his khaki shorts and his incredibly strong, hairy legs. At dinner I slid down from my chair and lay under the table and began to stroke the hairs on his legs. For a time he was polite, ignoring me, but then he complained to my mother that her son was stroking his legs. She made me sit up to eat but I'd lost all interest in food—I kept sliding back down into the darkness just to be near his legs. Eventually, they sent me to bed.

I knew "on the move." Let me explain. I was thirteen when my mother took my brother and me to Europe. On our first day in Amsterdam, we were touring in one of those long boats that cruise slowly up and down the canals. We got to the red light district, where girl prostitutes were showing their wares in the storefronts. Off in the distance, a shop came into view. In the window there was a life-size poster of a naked man; large red letters proclaimed: **"IT'S BINKY!"** Binky was a Dutch wet dream—blonde, lean, endowed, smiling. As the boat moved past the shop, my eyes stayed glued to Binky and I thought to myself, "I'm gay." It took all of two seconds. As if I had just said, "There goes a red Vespa." The rest of the summer had a new lens—tight pants on men in Italy, sweaty Spaniards in tiny bikinis—but with my newfound knowledge, I couldn't wait to return to my hometown—West Hollywood, California.

STEVE LEVITT

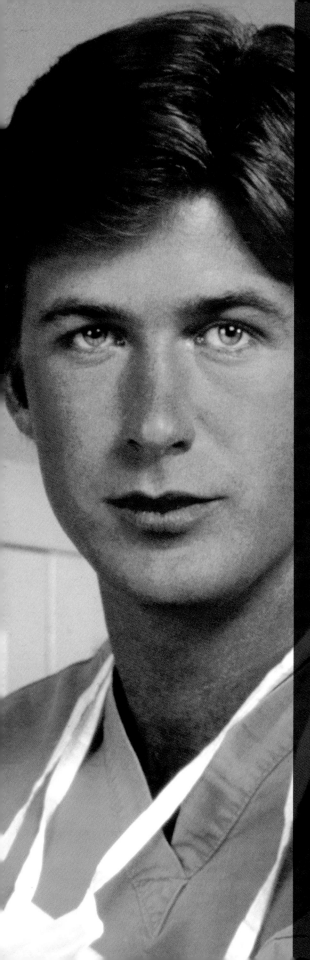

Q: What do you remember?
A: Well, one of my first acting
    jobs was on a short-lived
    TV show called *Cutter to
    Houston*, in 1983.
Q: What was it about?
A: Paramedics in helicopters.
    I played a kid who got hurt
    and had to be given mouth-
    to-mouth and carried to
    the waiting chopper by
    Dr. Hal Wexler.
Q: And?
A: I thought it was the greatest
    job I had ever gotten.
Q: Why?
A: Dr. Hal Wexler was
    played by Alec Baldwin.
Q: Got it.

CHAD ALLEN

When I was
IO

years old, I went to summer camp with a trunk full of soccer cleats and dreams of athletic prowess. Then I laid my eyes on the arts and crafts counselor—hairy legs, tight Lacoste shirt, and handlebar moustache. I immediately signed up for pottery class.

JONATHAN ADLER

Summer, 1981

I was at college and sick with the flu. The apartment I was renting had no cable, but somehow we were stealing HBO. All day I lay on the couch and was forced to watch tennis—Wimbledon to be exact. I hated sports; I was a theater major!

Martina Navratilova started playing.
I ignored my book.
I told my boyfriend I was busy when he called.

'62

My mother dressed me as
Little Red Riding Hood for
the Purim Festival—and I
never looked back. Tel Aviv, Israel

OFER KAMIL

'59

My sister dared me to wear her Little Red Riding Hood costume. From then on I realized clothes really *do* make the man! Akron, Ohio

SCOTT FRANK

117

I knew WHEN I saw the first kid get beaten up at school. WHEN I feared for Bambi's mother. WHEN Miss Gulch morphed into the cackling Wicked Witch of the West inside the twister. WHEN my babysitter Lori came over and put on the album *Goodbye Yellow Brick Road* and I heard the first notes of "Bennie and the Jets." WHEN I lay awake in my bed in the dark late on Sunday nights listening to Dr. Ruth

ANDY TOWLE

talk about erections and premature ejaculation. WHEN the boy from down the street came to mow the front lawn and finished in a cloud of hairy legs, sweat, and green grass clippings. WHEN at twelve I was mortified about approaching the counter at 7-Eleven to make my purchase: a *Gentleman's Quarterly*. WHEN I opened that magazine and saw Calvin Klein's first underwear ad, the bronzed god leaning back against a white pillar and azure sky. WHEN I saw Matt Dillon "do it for Johnny" in *The Outsiders*. WHEN I got my first spread-eagle glimpse of *Penthouse*... and felt nothing. WHEN I crashed riding my ten-speed down Keystone Avenue because I was distracted singing, "The hills are alive with the sound of music . . ." WHEN a school-mate spray-painted a jagged message on a town train overpass calling me a faggot and I snuck out in the middle of the night to paint over it so my parents wouldn't see it. WHEN Olivia Newton-John showed up in skin-tight leather at the carnival. WHEN the local bullies washed my face out with snow. WHEN I finally had sex with my high-school girlfriend to convince myself that "this was just a phase." WHEN he turned and kissed me on the hill behind campus and I felt his stubble on my face and it was like an anthem from the future singing yes, finally, finally you will know what it is to feel LOVE.

THANKS to Alice Martell,
Aliza Fogelson, Lynn Robb,
Rob Bragin, and Charlie Stratton.

Thanks to David Monahan for his
non-stop barrage of petty insults
and hard work.

Very special thanks to the men and
women who were kind, generous, and
secure enough to share their stories.